P9-CCQ-507

DINOSAURS WITH FEATHERS
The Ancestors of Modern Birds

by CAROLINE ARNOLD

illustrated by Laurie Caple

CLARION BOOKS ◆ NEW YORK

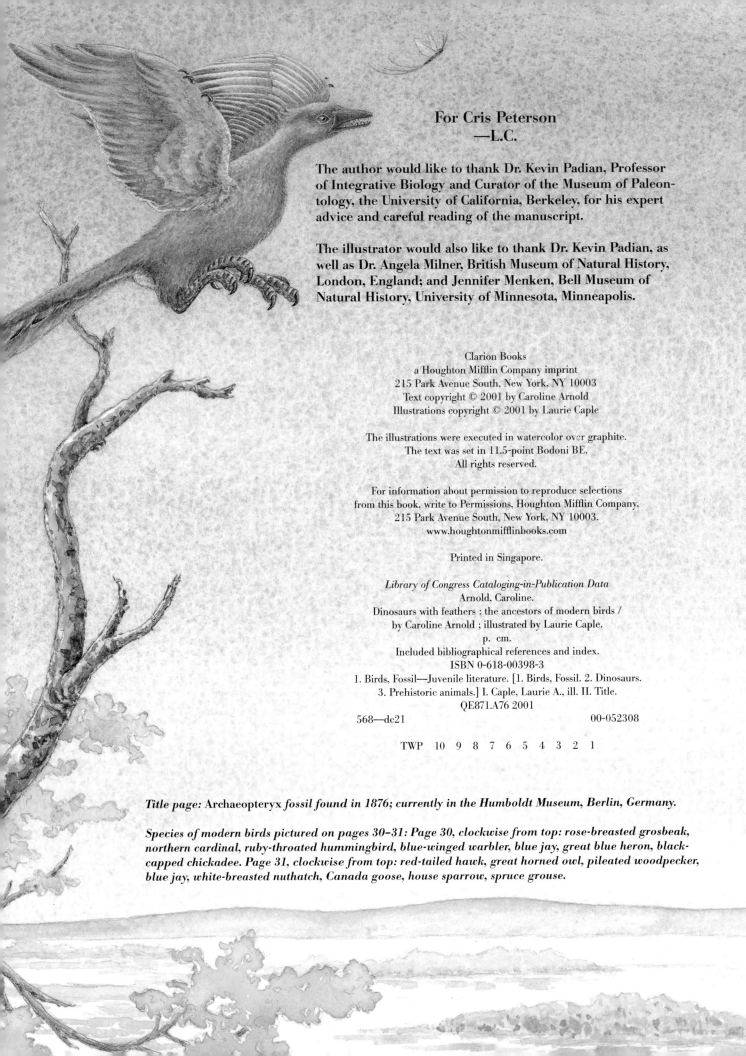

For Cris Peterson
—L.C.

The author would like to thank Dr. Kevin Padian, Professor of Integrative Biology and Curator of the Museum of Paleontology, the University of California, Berkeley, for his expert advice and careful reading of the manuscript.

The illustrator would also like to thank Dr. Kevin Padian, as well as Dr. Angela Milner, British Museum of Natural History, London, England; and Jennifer Menken, Bell Museum of Natural History, University of Minnesota, Minneapolis.

Clarion Books
a Houghton Mifflin Company imprint
215 Park Avenue South, New York, NY 10003
Text copyright © 2001 by Caroline Arnold
Illustrations copyright © 2001 by Laurie Caple

The illustrations were executed in watercolor over graphite.
The text was set in 11.5-point Bodoni BE.

For information about permission to reproduce selections
from this book, write to Permissions, Houghton Mifflin Company,
215 Park Avenue South, New York, NY 10003.
www.houghtonmifflinbooks.com

Printed in Singapore.

Library of Congress Cataloging-in-Publication Data
Arnold, Caroline.
Dinosaurs with feathers : the ancestors of modern birds /
by Caroline Arnold ; illustrated by Laurie Caple.
p. cm.
Included bibliographical references and index.
ISBN 0-618-00398-3
1. Birds, Fossil—Juvenile literature. [1. Birds, Fossil. 2. Dinosaurs.
3. Prehistoric animals.] I. Caple, Laurie A., ill. II. Title.
QE871.A76 2001
568—dc21   00-052308

TWP   10 9 8 7 6 5 4 3 2 1

Title page: Archaeopteryx fossil found in 1876; currently in the Humboldt Museum, Berlin, Germany.

Species of modern birds pictured on pages 30–31: Page 30, clockwise from top: rose-breasted grosbeak, northern cardinal, ruby-throated hummingbird, blue-winged warbler, blue jay, great blue heron, black-capped chickadee. Page 31, clockwise from top: red-tailed hawk, great horned owl, pileated woodpecker, blue jay, white-breasted nuthatch, Canada goose, house sparrow, spruce grouse.

CONTENTS

BIRDS IN THE AGE OF DINOSAURS

One hundred fifty million years ago, a crow-size bird glided on feather-covered wings across a tropical lagoon in what is now southern Germany. Along the lagoon's muddy shore dragonflies hovered, bees buzzed, and small meat-eating dinosaurs hunted for lizards. Sharing the sky with the bird were flying reptiles called pterosaurs (TARE-oh-sawrs), which soared on narrow, skin-covered wings. For some reason that we will never know, the bird did not complete its journey across the lagoon. Instead, it plunged into the water and died. It sank to the bottom, where fine-grained, chalky mud gently covered its body, almost perfectly preserving the delicate skeleton as well as an impression of feathers. There the bird lay, encased in its muddy tomb, until its discovery millions of years later.

The ancient bird lived during a period of the Earth's history called the Mesozoic Era, a time when dinosaurs were the dominant land animals. Scientists divide the Mesozoic Era into three periods: the Triassic, about 250 to 208 million years ago; the Jurassic, about 208 to 144 million years ago; and the Cretaceous, about 144 to 65 million years ago. The ancient bird that fell into the sea lived at the end of the Jurassic Period. During the Cretaceous Period that followed, there was a great expansion of bird species, ranging from sparrow-size tree dwellers to loon-like water birds. Recent fossil discoveries of ancient birds—and of dinosaurs that were their close relatives—are helping us to learn about the amazing diversity of life in the Mesozoic Era and how adaptations such as feathers may have helped some of these animals in their daily lives.

BURIED IN LIMESTONE

The lagoon in which the ancient bird was buried slowly dried up and the chalky deposits turned into limestone, a rock that people often use for building. Limestone that is especially fine-grained is used to make lithographic plates for printing. In 1861, workers in a lithographic limestone quarry near the small town of Solnhofen, Germany, cut a slab of rock and split it open. As they carefully examined each surface for imperfections, they discovered the imprint of feathers and tiny bones. Although they were accustomed to finding the remains of insects, fish, and even small dinosaurs embedded in the limestone, they had never seen a fossil like this one. It was the skeleton of an animal that resembled a small dinosaur—except that it had long feathers fanning out from its arms and tail. They had found the remains of the ancient bird.

The skeleton in the limestone slab was arranged in an almost lifelike pose. The bird's leg bones, one of which ended in a perfectly formed foot, were spread on either side of the long tail, and the arm bones were raised above the body. A long line of tiny vertebrae, as well as the feathers that extended outward from them, were clearly visible in the tail. Feathers also extended from the arms, making them into wings. Some of the bones, including those of the skull, had become detached and scattered, but the specimen was otherwise nearly complete and amazingly well preserved.

Scientists named the new fossil *Archaeopteryx* (ar-kee-OP-tuh-ricks) from Greek words meaning "ancient wing." This remarkable discovery provided the first clear proof that birds had been alive in the Age of Dinosaurs. *Archaeopteryx* is still the oldest known bird.

Only seven fossil skeletons and one feather imprint of *Archaeopteryx* have ever been found. The original 1861 discovery is on exhibit at the British Museum of Natural History in London. The best preserved *Archaeopteryx* fossil was unearthed in 1876 in a quarry not far from Solnhofen. It is on display at the Humboldt Museum of Natural History in Berlin. In this specimen even the skull of the bird is clearly visible, as are the clawed wings and toes.

The Archaeopteryx *fossil discovered in the Solnhofen quarry was about 22 inches high.*

BIRD FOSSILS

The remains of ancient birds are extremely rare because their small, delicate bones are often crushed or scattered before they can fossilize. The preservation of feathers is even rarer. When an animal dies, its soft body parts usually rot before they can be preserved. In most cases only the bones and other hard body parts, such as teeth and claws, become fossils. And this can happen only if they are buried quickly and protected from the weather and other destructive elements.

A fossil is any trace or remains of ancient life. It may be part of a plant or animal that has been preserved unchanged, or one whose structure has been replaced with minerals. A fossil may also be made when a plant or animal leaves an impression, or imprint, in mud or fine sand that later becomes preserved as stone.

In the century following the discovery of *Archaeopteryx*, few bird fossils were found. In recent years, however, there has been a flurry of discoveries. Even more exciting has been the unearthing of dinosaur fossils that show that some of these reptiles had feathers just like birds. Fossils of ancient birds and of dinosaurs with birdlike features have been found in China, Spain, Argentina, Madagascar, the United States, Canada, and elsewhere. These new discoveries are helping to answer many questions about prehistoric birds and their possible relatives.

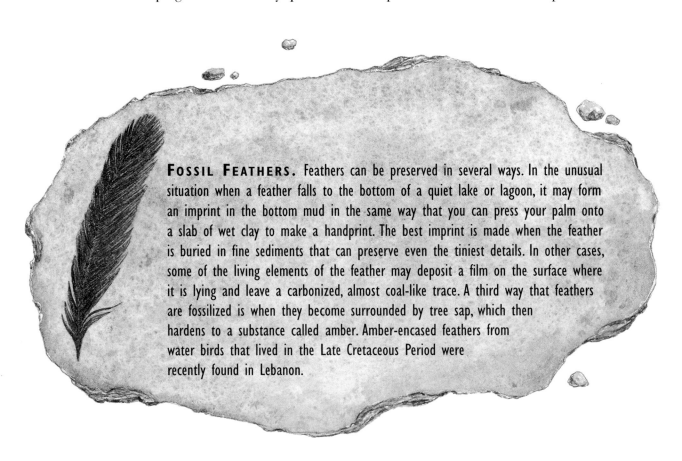

FOSSIL FEATHERS. Feathers can be preserved in several ways. In the unusual situation when a feather falls to the bottom of a quiet lake or lagoon, it may form an imprint in the bottom mud in the same way that you can press your palm onto a slab of wet clay to make a handprint. The best imprint is made when the feather is buried in fine sediments that can preserve even the tiniest details. In other cases, some of the living elements of the feather may deposit a film on the surface where it is lying and leave a carbonized, almost coal-like trace. A third way that feathers are fossilized is when they become surrounded by tree sap, which then hardens to a substance called amber. Amber-encased feathers from water birds that lived in the Late Cretaceous Period were recently found in Lebanon.

*Sinosauropteryx is a dinosaur that lived in China 120 million years ago.
It had a bristly, featherlike coat.*

*Rahonavis is a bird that lived on Madagascar 70 million years ago.
A sharp, curved claw on its second toe is remarkably similar to that
of the predatory dinosaur Velociraptor.*

Archaeopteryx's pointed teeth were good for grasping insects such as dragonflies.

ARCHAEOPTERYX — HALF BIRD, HALF REPTILE

Archaeopteryx was recognized as a bird because it had feathers and looked as if it could fly. Yet in many ways it was quite unbirdlike and had features more typically found in reptiles. Instead of a toothless beak, *Archaeopteryx* had a jaw lined with sharp, cone-shaped teeth. Like most small reptiles, *Archaeopteryx* probably ate insects. Fossils of cicadas, dragonflies, and wood wasps were among the many insects embedded in the limestone deposits where *Archaeopteryx* was found.

Archaeopteryx was unlike most living birds in that it had three bony claws on each of its wings, just like the claws on a dinosaur's hand. These may have been used for grasping branches when climbing trees, but they were more likely used to hold prey and tear apart things. Another reptilian feature of *Archaeopteryx* was its long bony tail. It had two feathers connected to each vertebra of its tail.

There has been much debate about how well *Archaeopteryx* could fly and how it could get itself aloft. Possibly it launched itself from trees or rocks. Or it may have leaped into the air from the ground. Recently, two specialists in aerodynamics and fossil birds showed that *Archaeopteryx* could have developed enough speed to take off by running along the ground and flapping its wings. At the American Museum of Natural History in New York, you can see a realistic, life-size model of *Archaeopteryx* poised for takeoff.

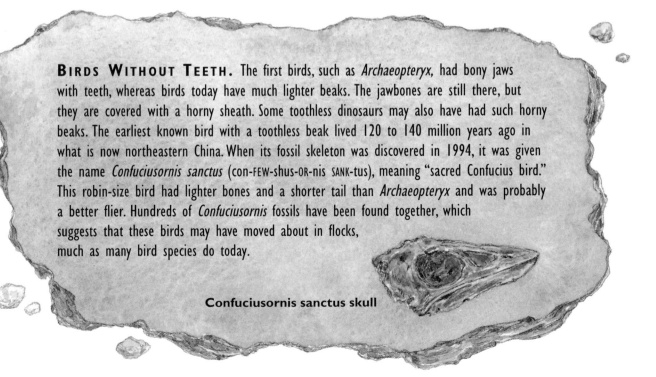

BIRDS WITHOUT TEETH. The first birds, such as *Archaeopteryx,* had bony jaws with teeth, whereas birds today have much lighter beaks. The jawbones are still there, but they are covered with a horny sheath. Some toothless dinosaurs may also have had such horny beaks. The earliest known bird with a toothless beak lived 120 to 140 million years ago in what is now northeastern China. When its fossil skeleton was discovered in 1994, it was given the name *Confuciusornis sanctus* (con-FEW-shus-OR-nis SANK-tus), meaning "sacred Confucius bird." This robin-size bird had lighter bones and a shorter tail than *Archaeopteryx* and was probably a better flier. Hundreds of *Confuciusornis* fossils have been found together, which suggests that these birds may have moved about in flocks, much as many bird species do today.

Confuciusornis sanctus skull

THE ANCESTORS OF BIRDS

One way that scientists learn about ancient birds and their relatives is by examining fossil skeletons and noting the similarities and differences. They also compare fossilized remains with living birds and other animals. Species that are closely related often share many unusual features. These features have been inherited from a common ancestor. Shared features don't always mean that two animals are related—for instance, both birds and bats can fly, but a bat is a mammal. However, when two animals have a large number of unusual or uniquely shared features, they are likely to have a common heritage. The system of classifying animals according to their shared inherited characteristics is called cladistics.

Inherited characteristics are passed from parents to their offspring through their genes. Genes, which are made of tiny strands of DNA, are found within each body cell. They are a set of instructions for the growth and functioning of the body. Every living thing has its own unique set of genes. Sometimes genes change, or mutate, to create a new trait, which is then passed on to the next generation. Over time, a combination of new inherited traits can result in a new species. The new species shares most traits with its ancestors, but it also has new features.

Birds, along with crocodiles, dinosaurs, pterosaurs, and some other extinct reptiles, belong to a group of reptiles called archosaurs (AR-koh-sawrs). The first archosaurs appeared around 225 million years ago, about 10 million years before the oldest known dinosaur. Archosaurs are distinguished by a hole in the skull between the eye and nasal openings. Their teeth are set in deep sockets.

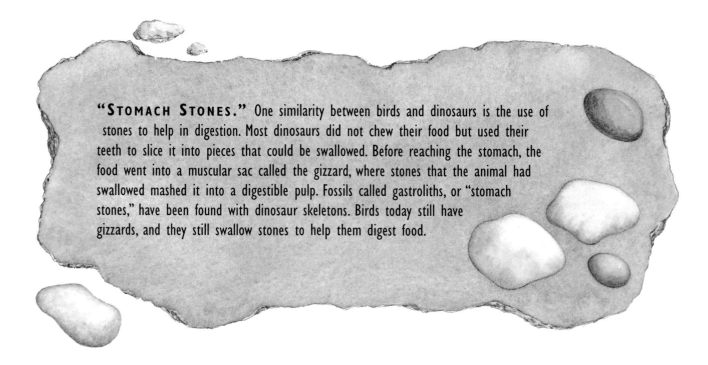

"STOMACH STONES." One similarity between birds and dinosaurs is the use of stones to help in digestion. Most dinosaurs did not chew their food but used their teeth to slice it into pieces that could be swallowed. Before reaching the stomach, the food went into a muscular sac called the gizzard, where stones that the animal had swallowed mashed it into a digestible pulp. Fossils called gastroliths, or "stomach stones," have been found with dinosaur skeletons. Birds today still have gizzards, and they still swallow stones to help them digest food.

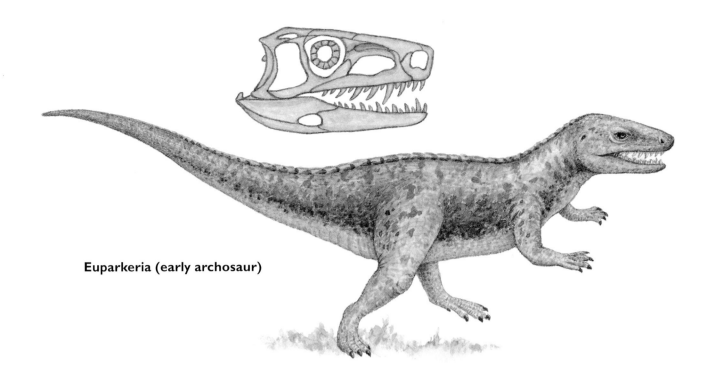

Euparkeria (early archosaur)

Rhamphorhynchus (pterosaur)

Tyrannosaurus (dinosaur)

Archaeopteryx (early bird)

Teleosaurus (early crocodile)

THEROPOD DINOSAURS

From the time of the first dinosaur discoveries in the middle of the nineteenth century, people have recognized that dinosaurs and birds had a number of common traits. Like other reptiles, both have scaly skin—birds have scales on their legs and feet—and both reproduce by laying eggs. Dinosaurs and birds also have many similar skeletal features.

In looking for close relatives of ancient birds, scientists have focused on a group of dinosaurs called theropods. Theropods were agile, mostly meat-eating dinosaurs that walked on two legs. They ranged in size from the giant *Tyrannosaurus rex* (ty-RAN-uh-sawr-us rex) to small, chicken-size dinosaurs like *Compsognathus* (komp-sug-NAY-thus). *Compsognathus* lived at the same time and in the same environment as *Archaeopteryx*. Their skeletons are so similar that two fossils once thought to belong to *Compsognathus* were later correctly identified as being those of *Archaeopteryx*. Dinosaurs with the most similarities to birds are found within a group of small theropods called dromaeosaurs (DRO-mee-oh-sawrs), whose name means "swift-running."

Among the many skeletal features that theropods have in common with birds are bone structure and muscles for walking on two legs; two- or three-fingered hands; three forward-facing toes; and hollow, thin-walled bones. Adaptations such as these helped the theropod dinosaurs to be more effective predators. These same features made the evolution of flight possible for early birds.

SKELETAL FEATURE	THEROPODS	BIRDS
Two-legged posture	Good for running and leaping; freed hands for grasping	Good for running and leaping; freed arms lengthened and became wings
Two- or three-fingered hands	Used for grasping and holding prey	Fingers became longer and joined to support end of wing
Three-toed feet	Gripped the ground when running	Front toes grip the ground when running; in most birds a fourth toe in back allows them to perch
Thin-walled bones	Made a lighter skeleton	Lightweight bones make it easier to fly; air sacs in the bones help birds breathe more efficiently

Tyrannosaurus rex

Dromaeosaurus

15

WISHBONES

When *Archaeopteryx* was first discovered, one of the skeletal features that clearly identified it as a bird was its furcula, or wishbone, a boomerang-shaped bone at the front of the chest connected to the breastbone. The furcula is the equivalent of the two collarbones in other vertebrates, but in birds the two sides are joined in the middle. The muscles that lift a bird's wings are attached to the breastbone, and the furcula, which is flexible in some birds, can act as a spring that helps conserve energy during flight.

For many years it was widely thought that dinosaurs did not have furculas and that this was a feature that separated dinosaurs and birds. Then, in 1991, the fossil skeleton of a theropod dinosaur with a boomerang-shaped furcula was found in the Gobi Desert. The skeleton was that of *Velociraptor* (ve-LOS-ih-rap-tor), or "swift robber." The furcula of this ferocious predator helped strengthen the skeleton in the upper part of its body. Since that discovery, furculas have been found in other theropod dinosaurs as well, including allosaurs, tyrannosaurs, and oviraptorids.

Great horned owl

wishbone

Velociraptor

wishbone

Archaeopteryx

wishbone

WRISTBONES

Another feature once thought to be unique to birds is a small, half-moon-shaped bone in the wrist that enables a bird to swing its wrist joint forward and backward. This motion gives the bird's wingstroke thrust, which propels it forward. In 1964, a theropod dinosaur was found that had a similar half-moon-shaped bone. It was *Deinonychus* (die-NON-ih-kus), or "terrible claw." This swift-moving dinosaur ran after its prey and grabbed it with its clawed hands. Its crescent-shaped wristbones allowed its hands to move both up and down and from side to side, and made them more effective for catching prey. *Deinonychus* lived about 115 million years ago in what is now Montana.

A bird's wings are its arms, and when a bird flies, it moves its arms up and down from its shoulders. Most dinosaurs couldn't do this, but *Deinonychus* and other dromaeosaurs could. They may have spread out their arms for balance as they ran on their long legs. The discoveries of shared features in *Velociraptor*, *Deinonychus*, and birds have added support to the idea that they are closely related.

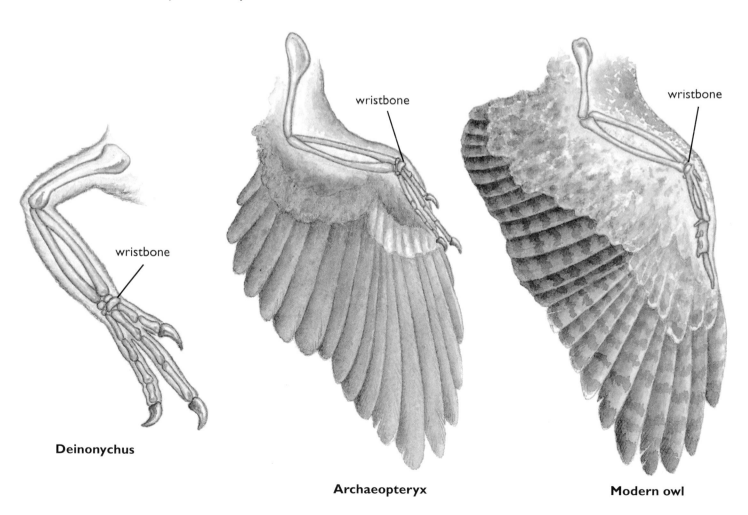

Deinonychus

wristbone

Archaeopteryx

wristbone

Modern owl

wristbone

DINOSAURS WITH FEATHERS

One characteristic unique to all living birds is feathers. No other living thing has them. Yet if birds are descended from dinosaurs, one would expect that some dinosaurs had feathers, too. Feathers grow from structures in the skin similar to the structures that develop into scales in reptiles and fur or hair in mammals.

In 1996, scientists announced the discovery of a new dinosaur called *Sinosauropteryx prima* (SINE-oh-sawr-OP-tuh-ricks PREE-ma), or "first Chinese dragon feather." Found in Liaoning Province in northeastern China, the fossil bones of this one-foot-tall, long-tailed theropod were surrounded by an impression of hairlike filaments. It was clear that the dinosaur had worn a bristly, featherlike coat. These were not true feathers, but they may have been structures from which feathers evolved. Since then, another specimen of *Sinosauropteryx* has been found, with the same filaments all over its body. *Sinosauropteryx* is closely related to *Compsognathus*, the small dinosaur that lived with *Archaeopteryx*.

In 1997, a second kind of feathered dinosaur was discovered in the same location. It was given the name *Protarchaeopteryx* (pro-tar-kee-OP-tuh-ricks). It had short, true feathers on its body, long, symmetrical feathers on its hands, and longer feathers attached to its tail. This turkey-size animal was similar in many ways to *Archaeopteryx*, but it was not as bird-like. It could not fly, because its wings and feathers were too small in proportion to its body. This fossil and other recent discoveries support the growing conviction that feathers may have been common among the theropod dinosaurs.

Sinosauropteryx prima

Protarchaeopteryx

THE AMAZING CHINESE FOSSILS

Some of the most spectacular fossils of the Early Cretaceous Period have come from Liaoning Province. About 120 million years ago, this now arid region was covered by lush vegetation and supported an abundance of wildlife. The idyllic scene came to an abrupt end when a large volcano to the west exploded in a violent eruption and filled the air with poisonous gas. A great many living things died instantly, and many sank to the bottom of a small lake, where they were gradually buried in ash and silt. This site has become a treasure trove for paleontologists. Millions of fossils have been excavated from the former lake bottom, including many early birds and several feathered dinosaurs. They provide us with a window into a moment in time when some dinosaurs had birdlike features and some of the earliest birds were taking to the skies. Recently discovered feathered dinosaurs from China include *Caudipteryx zoui* (caw-DIP-tuh-ricks ZOO-ee), *Sinornithosaurus millenii* (sine-OR-nith-oh-sawr-us mi-LEN-ee-ee), and *Beipiaosaurus inexpectus* (bay-pee-OW-sawr-us in-ex-PEK-tus).

Caudipteryx zoui, whose first name means "tail feathers," was a long-legged theropod. It was a speedy runner, but it could not fly. It had small plumelike feathers on its body like *Protarchaeopteryx*, as well as filaments like those of *Sinosauropteryx*. It also had a spray of feathers on its hands and large plumes on its tail. Though these features were birdlike, its short arms, serrated teeth, and other characteristics made its body more like that of a dinosaur. It is related to *Oviraptor* (OH-vih-rap-tor), a theropod from Mongolia.

Sinornithosaurus millenii was a fierce-looking animal that had teeth and claws like a dinosaur and shoulder bones and a wishbone, or furcula, like a bird. It could not fly, although it may have leaped into the air in pursuit of prey. It may have hunted lizards and small mammals. This eagle-size dinosaur was a type of dromaeosaur. It has been found with filament-like skin coverings but not true feathers.

Beipiaosaurus inexpectus, which was seven feet long, is the largest feathered dinosaur yet discovered. Like *Sinornithosaurus*, it had a covering of filaments but not true feathers. Stiff, narrow filaments, up to two inches long, extended from its forearms. This long-necked, long-clawed dinosaur is a type of theropod called a therizinosaur (ther-ih-ZINE-oh-sawr). These large slow-moving theropods may have been plant eaters. They would have been too heavy to fly.

Some theropods, like *Caudipteryx* and *Protarchaeopteryx*, had true feathers as well as filaments. Other theropods, such as *Sinosauropteryx, Beipiaosaurus*, and *Sinornithosaurus*, seem to have had only filaments. However, it is possible that they, too, had true feathers—they just haven't been found yet.

Beipiaosaurus inexpectus

Sinornithosaurus millenii

Caudipteryx zoui

WHY FEATHERS?

Dinosaurs were reptiles, and in today's world, reptiles are cold-blooded animals. Their body temperature changes with that of their surroundings. Birds, on the other hand, are warm-blooded and can maintain a constant body temperature even when the temperature of the surrounding environment changes. Were some dinosaurs warm-blooded, too? Maybe. At higher temperatures, many chemical processes in the body can run faster, so the animals are more active. If dinosaurs were warm-blooded, they probably had more rapid growth rates and more active lifestyles than other reptiles.

Producing body heat requires energy, so an animal with an outer covering that prevents heat loss can save energy. Perhaps that is partly why some dinosaurs had feathers. Soft down feathers trap air next to the skin and act like an insulating blanket. For small dinosaurs, feathers that helped them stay warm would have been especially important because their bodies would have cooled off much more quickly than those of the big dinosaurs. Even if the big dinosaurs didn't need feathers to stay warm, their small babies in the nest might have had coats of down.

Dinosaurs might also have used feathers for display, just as birds do today. That could be why several of the Chinese dinosaurs had feathers on their arms and tails. Colorful or unusually shaped feathers would have helped them attract mates or impress rivals. Feathers might also have provided camouflage, helping them to sneak up on prey or hide to avoid being preyed upon.

The use of feathers for flight probably came after their use for insulation or display. As some dinosaurs became smaller and evolved longer arms and more specialized feathers, they developed the ability to fly.

FEATHERS FOR FLYING

We don't know how the ancestors of birds first started to fly. They might have climbed up trees or to the top of other tall places, jumped off, and then glided to the ground with the help of their feathered arms. Another possibility is that they ran along the ground and leaped into the air after insects or to escape from predators. As they stretched out their arms for balance, they may have flown or glided for short distances. Most likely it was a combination of jumping and leaping that helped the earliest birds develop their flying abilities. Then, with improvements in their feathers and other adaptations, they eventually became accomplished in the air. Their feathered arms became wings capable of powered flight.

When a bird flies, air moves across the curved shape of each wing from front to back. This creates unequal air pressure above and below, and helps lift the bird into the air. The power for flight comes from the downstroke of the wing, which must move the bird forward fast enough to create the lift necessary to overcome the pull of gravity.

flight feathers

Archaeopteryx
(ancient bird)

flight feathers

Great blue heron
(modern bird)

WING FEATHERS. The feathers that are most important for flying are the long feathers on a bird's wings. Like the contour feathers that cover the body, each flight feather has a long hollow shaft at its center. Along the shaft are thin strands that are hooked together to give the feather its smooth, connected surface. Flight feathers are asymmetrically shaped—the narrower edge faces the front of the wing and the wider portion faces the back. Each one is like a mini-wing and provides additional lift during flight. All living birds that fly have asymmetrical flight feathers. So did *Archaeopteryx* and other early birds.

pygostyle

**Oviraptorosaur
(dinosaur)**

**Spruce grouse
(modern bird)**

TAIL FEATHERS. Birds use their tail feathers for steering and maneuvering while flying. In living birds these feathers are supported by or anchored in a bone called the pygostyle (PIE-go-stile). The earliest birds, such as *Archaeopteryx*, did not have pygostyles and probably could not maneuver as well in the air as modern birds. Recently, the fossil bones of a type of dinosaur known as an oviraptorosaur, or "egg stealer," were unearthed in Mongolia. What was unusual about this ostrich-size feathered dinosaur was that the last vertebrae had fused to form a pygostyle. It is possible that this bone supported long tail feathers like those of its relative, *Caudipteryx*. Because the oviraptorosaur was too big to fly, it may have used its tail feathers for display, just as many modern birds do.

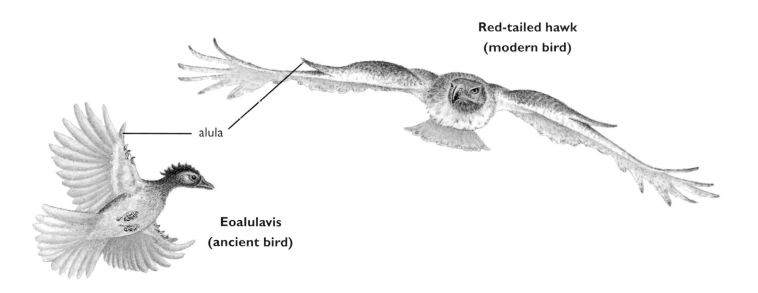

**Red-tailed hawk
(modern bird)**

alula

**Eoalulavis
(ancient bird)**

THUMB FEATHERS. Living birds have tufts of feathers attached to the part of the wing that is the equivalent of the bird's thumb. This tuft, or "little wing," is called the alula (AL-you-luh) and gives a bird control and maneuverability when flying at low speeds. The alula, which can be raised above the rest of the wing, works like the wing flap on an airplane to break up turbulence around the wing and allows the bird to slow down in the air without stalling. The earliest birds did not have alulas. Recently, the remains of a bird that lived 115 million years ago were found in Spain. It is the oldest known example of a bird with an alula. Named *Eoalulavis* (EE-oh-al-you-LAY-vis), this fossil shows that by the middle of the Cretaceous Period birds had developed flying abilities nearly as sophisticated as those of birds today.

BEYOND SKELETONS

In addition to fossil bones, other clues to the habits and lifestyles of ancient birds include ancient trackways and preserved eggs.

Bird tracks are distinctive because of their small size and their three- or four-toed shape. Footprints can tell us much about a bird's movements, how fast it is going, its habits, and where it lives. They also contain information about a bird's size and shape as well as its way of life. Prints that show a partly webbed foot, for example, indicate a bird that lives in or near water. Perching birds generally hop on the ground with their feet side by side. Game birds usually walk or run and have prints with an alternate pattern of steps.

It is difficult to distinguish between bird trackways and the tracks of small three-toed dinosaurs. Bird tracks are usually small, but so are those of young dinosaurs. Bird tracks often have a prominent toe print that points backward, but some theropod tracks made in deep mud also show a backward-facing toe. The earliest well-accepted fossil bird tracks are from the Late Cretaceous Period.

Fossilized bird eggs are extremely rare. The only known eggs from dinosaur times are from the Cretaceous Period and were found in the Gobi Desert. They are of a bird called *Gobipipus* (go-bee-PIPE-us). Each egg is about 1½ inches long and ¾ inch wide, about half the size of a chicken egg. Some of the shells contain skeletons of growing birds. The well-developed bones suggest that the young birds would have been able to fly soon after hatching.

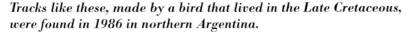

Tracks like these, made by a bird that lived in the Late Cretaceous, were found in 1986 in northern Argentina.

Fossil Gobipipus eggs, found clustered in what appeared to be a nest, were embedded in the soil with the pointed end down.

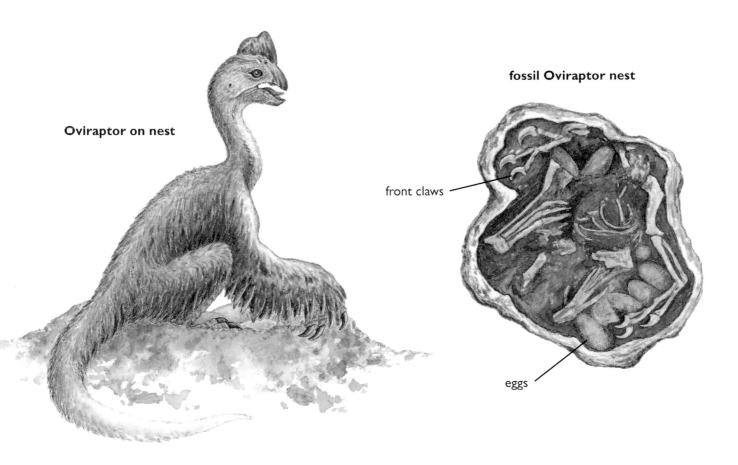

Oviraptor on nest

fossil Oviraptor nest

front claws

eggs

Another recent find in the Gobi Desert was the skeleton and nest of an Oviraptor, positioned as if the dinosaur was sitting on the eggs, much the way today's birds do. This discovery suggests that another behavior shared by birds and dinosaurs is the brooding, or incubating, of eggs.

FOSSIL BIRDS OF THE CRETACEOUS

During the Cretaceous Period there was a great diversity of birds. One large group, whose fossil remains were first discovered in northwest Argentina in 1975, is called the Enantithornithes (ee-nan-tith-OR-nith-eez). They ranged from sparrow size to vulture size, lived in many parts of the world, and were both tree and ground dwellers. Many of them were strong fliers. They were the most common land birds of Mesozoic times.

Hesperornis (hes-per-OR-nis) was one of a group of large flightless birds that spent most of their lives in the water. These birds had forelimbs too small for flying, and the angled position of their legs probably made them quite clumsy on land. Like loons and grebes today, they were excellent divers and used their webbed feet to propel themselves through the water. These fish eaters captured prey in their long toothed jaws.

Ichthyornis (ick-thee-OR-nis) and its relatives were another type of toothed water bird. These tern-size birds lived along shorelines but often flew out over lakes and inland seas to look for fish. Many fossil bones of both *Hesperornis* and *Ichthyornis* have been found in rocks that were once at the bottom of a large inland sea covering much of central North America. These birds are known from other parts of the world as well.

An unusual bird, discovered in the mid-1980s in Argentina, is *Patagopteryx* (pat-uh-GOP-tuh-ricks). This sturdy rooster-size bird had wings so small that it couldn't have flown. Like kiwis and other flightless birds today, it was a ground dweller. Some other groups of birds whose descendants are living today, including shore birds, water birds, ground birds, and even parrots, were also present in the Late Cretaceous.

The end of the Cretaceous Period was marked by the extinction of the dinosaurs, whose numbers had been declining for many years. Other forms of Mesozoic life perished at this time as well, including some groups of ancient birds. Yet many groups of birds clearly managed to survive. They not only thrived but diversified into the many groups whose descendants are among the nearly 10,000 species of birds that populate the world today.

Hesperornis

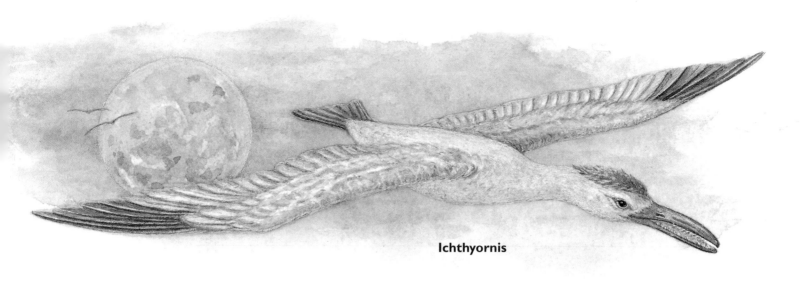

Ichthyornis

Patagopteryx

Sinornis
(Enantithornithes group)

TODAY'S BIRDS—ARE THEY DINOSAURS IN DISGUISE?

The recent discoveries of feathered dinosaurs, along with previously known similarities between theropods and birds, make it clear that birds are the descendants of theropod dinosaurs. The evidence indicates that sometime in the middle of the Mesozoic Era one small group of theropods evolved the ability to fly—and thus became birds. These early birds shared many characteristics with theropods that did not fly. These shared features show that they are closely related.

Because birds evolved from theropod dinosaurs, most scientists now consider birds as a subgroup of dinosaurs, in the same way that carnivorous mammals such as cats, dogs, and bears are considered a subgroup of mammals. Just as cats and dogs can be both carnivores and mammals, sparrows and bluejays can be both birds and dinosaurs. This is why we can now say that dinosaurs did not become entirely extinct.

Much remains to be learned about the earliest birds, but as more evidence about them and their ancient ancestors emerges, we are getting a better understanding of how birds began and of their true relationship with dinosaurs. The early history of birds is a long and complicated story that still has many missing pieces. Known fossils are only a tiny sample of the abundance of life in prehistoric times. New fossils are changing our views both about birds and about the appearance and lifestyles of dinosaurs. It may be that some dinosaurs were as flamboyant as peacocks and that others nurtured fuzzy babies in the nest.

Amazing as it may seem, as we look at the sparrows and bluejays in our backyards today, we are seeing tiny dinosaurs in disguise.

FOR FURTHER INFORMATION

Ackerman, Jennifer. "Dinosaurs Take Wing." *National Geographic* (July 1998): 74–99.

Dinosaurs and Their Living Relatives. London: The British Museum, 1979, 1985.

Freedman, Russell. *How Birds Fly*. New York: Holiday House, 1977.

Simons, Lewis M. "Fossil Trail." *National Geographic* (October 2000): 128–132.

Sloan, Christopher P. *Feathered Dinosaurs*. Washington, D.C.: National Geographic Society, 2000.

———. "Feathers for T. Rex?" *National Geographic* (November 1999): 98–107.

INDEX

Page numbers in **bold** type refer to illustrations.